OGRAPHIES

ROSA PARKS

by Lakita Wilson

PEBBLE
a capstone imprint

Pebble Explore is published by Pebble, an imprint of Capstone.
1710 Roe Crest Drive, North Mankato, Minnesota 56003
www.capstonepub.com

**Library of Congress Cataloging-in-Publication data is available
on the Library of Congress website.**
ISBN: 978-1-9771-1362-7 (library binding)
ISBN: 978-1-9771-1806-6 (paperback)
ISBN: 978-1-9771-1370-2 (eBook PDF)

Summary: Explores the life, challenges, and accomplishments of Rosa Parks,
a leader in the civil rights movement.

Image Credits
Alamy: Photo 12, 13; Getty Images: Bettmann, 9, The LIFE Images Collection/
Don Cravens, 18, 19; Library of Congress, Prints & Photographs Division:
NYWT&S Collection, #LC-USZ62-109426, 21, #LC-USZ62-109643, 16, Visual
Materials from the Rosa Parks Papers, #LC-DIG-ppmsca-38464, cover,
1, #LC-DIG-ppmsca-38927, 11, #LC-DIG-ppmsca-47044, 29, #LC-DIG-
ppmsca-47948, 23, #LC-DIG-ppmsca-48026, 25, #LC-DIG-ppmsca-48335,
7; Newscom: Reuters/Rebecca Cook, 27, Reuters/William Philpott, 5, SIPA/
Trippett, 26, Universal Images Group/Underwood Archives, 15; Shutterstock:
Curly Pat (geometric background), cover, back cover, 2, 29

Rosa Parks' name and image used with permission from The Rosa and
Raymond Parks Institute for Self Development.

Editorial Credits
Erika L. Shores, editor; Elyse White, designer; Svetlana Zhurkin,
media researcher; Katy LaVigne, production specialist

All internet sites appearing in back matter were available and accurate when
this book was sent to press.

Printed and bound in China.
2489

Table of Contents

Words in **bold** are in the glossary.

Who Was Rosa Parks?

Rosa Parks had a soft voice. But that did not stop her from saying what she knew was important. Rosa lived at a time when some **laws** were unfair. There were rules that kept black and white people apart. Rosa wanted black people to be treated the same as white people.

Almost 65 years ago, Rosa did not give up her bus seat to a white person. This led to changes in how black people were treated in the United States.

Childhood

Rosa Louise McCauley was born more than 105 years ago in 1913. Rosa and her family lived in Alabama.

Rosa learned at an early age about fairness. Rosa's mom told her to say "no" or "I prefer not" when something was unfair. Rosa's grandpa told her stories about people who hurt black people because of their skin color.

Rosa's mother, Leona Edwards McCauley

In the early 1900s, many states had laws to keep black and white people apart. The laws kept them apart in stores, at movies, and many other places.

White kids and black kids had to go to different schools. White kids in Rosa's town went to a big brick school. Black kids went to a small one-room school. It did not have windows.

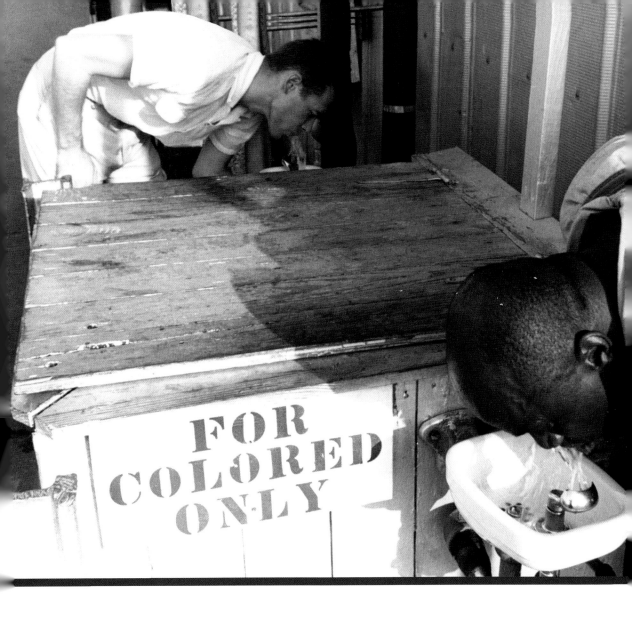

Rosa and other black people had to
use water fountains marked "colored."
Rosa wondered if the "whites only"
fountains had better water.

At age 11, Rosa went to a school for girls. They learned to cook and sew. Teachers talked about **self-respect**. They wanted the girls to know their brown skin didn't make them less important than anyone else.

At age 19, Rosa met and married Raymond Parks. They lived in Montgomery, Alabama. Raymond worked for the **rights** of black people. He wanted fair laws for them. He helped Rosa do this work too.

Raymond Parks

Adulthood

Rosa worked on **voting** rights for black people. People vote so they can decide on laws and leaders. At the time, people had to take a test to vote. The test was often unfair to black people. Rosa had to take it three times before she could vote.

In 1945, Rosa voted for the first time. She then helped other black people get to vote. Even though they could vote, many laws were still unfair. One law said black people had to sit in the back of city buses, and Rosa was tired of it.

Rosa Stays Put

On December 1, 1955, Rosa got on a city bus after work. She sat down in the only open bus seat. A white man got on the bus next. No seats were left for him in the rows for white people.

The bus driver looked at the first four rows of the colored section. He told the people in those seats to stand. Everyone else got up. But Rosa did not.

Rosa poses in a bus seat in 1956.

Rosa being fingerprinted

At the next stop, the police got on the bus. They asked Rosa to get up. She thought about what her mother had told her. Rosa was calm. She said "no." She was taken to jail.

Rosa went to **court** four days later on December 5, 1955. The court said she broke the law. She was told to pay $14.

Many black people in Montgomery
knew why Rosa did not stand that day.
They were tired of unfair laws too.

Black people stopped riding city buses. They wanted their **boycott** to show other people that keeping black and white people apart was wrong. People walked to work. Others drove groups in their cars. Some buses stopped running. Too few people were riding them.

People heard about the boycott on TV and the radio. They saw how unfair these laws were to black people. Black leaders spoke out on **civil rights**. Finally, on November 13, 1956, the U.S. **Supreme Court** said the law to keep black and white people apart on city buses must end.

The bus boycott changed Rosa's life. She lost her job. Angry people called her. Rosa and Raymond moved north to Detroit, Michigan. Rosa and Raymond hoped they would be safer there.

Later Life

Rosa and Raymond found out Detroit had problems too. There were few jobs. Schools were in bad shape. Black people were still treated badly.

Rosa went to work for John Conyers. He worked in the U.S. **Congress**. Conyers's job was to help people in Michigan. Rosa helped him work for better housing and schools in the areas where many black people lived.

John Conyers
and Rosa

Rosa spoke out for civil rights in other places. In 1984, South Africa still had laws keeping black and white people apart. Rosa joined a **protest** on December 10, 1984. The protesters wanted U.S. leaders to help black people in South Africa.

Rosa didn't stop there. In 1987, she started a group in Detroit that teaches young people about civil rights.

In 1990, Rosa met with students taking part in the group she started to teach about civil rights.

Remembering Rosa

Rosa has been **honored** in many ways. When Rosa was 83, she was given a medal by the U.S. president. Four years later, the Rosa Parks Museum and Library opened. It is in Montgomery.

In 2005, Rosa died at age 92. Black
ribbons were put on the front seats
of city buses in Montgomery and Detroit.
People stood along a street in Detroit.
They stood up for a woman who
refused to stand for unfair treatment.

Important Dates

February 4, 1913 — Rosa Louise McCauley is born in Tuskegee, Alabama.

1921 — Rosa moves to Montgomery, Alabama.

December 18, 1932 — Rosa marries Raymond Parks.

1945 — Rosa votes for the first time.

December 1, 1955 — Rosa does not give a white man her seat on a city bus. She is taken to jail.

December 5, 1955 — Rosa goes to court.

November 13, 1956 — The U.S. Supreme Court says that keeping black and white people apart on buses is no longer allowed.

December 21, 1956 — The bus boycott ends after the U.S. Supreme Court's decision is made into law.

1957 — Rosa and Raymond move to Detroit.

September 9, 1996 — Rosa is given the Presidential Medal of Freedom.

December 1, 2000 — The Rosa Parks Museum and Library opens in Montgomery.

October 24, 2005 — Rosa Parks dies at the age of 92.

Fast Facts

Name:
Rosa Parks

Role:
civil rights leader

Life dates:
February 4, 1913 to October 24, 2005

Key accomplishments:
Rosa did not give up her bus seat to a white man. Her action helped end unfair laws keeping black and white people apart. She went on to spend her life helping black people.

Glossary

boycott (BOY-kot)—to refuse to buy, use, or go to, in order to make a protest or bring about a change

civil rights (SI-vil RYTS)—freedoms everyone should have

Congress (KAHNG-gruhs)—the government body of the United States that makes laws, made up of the Senate and the House of Representatives

court (KORT)—the place where laws are carried out

honor (ON-ur)—to give praise or show respect

law (LAW)—a rule made by a government that must be followed

protest (pro-TEST)—to speak out about something strongly and publicly

right (RYT)—something that everyone should be able to do or to have and that the government shouldn't be able to take away, such as the right to speak freely

self-respect (SELF-ri-SPEKT)—to show concern and care for oneself

Supreme Court (suh-PREEM KORT)—the most powerful court in the United States

vote (VOHT)—to make a choice

Read More

Lewis Patrick, Denise. *A Girl Named Rosa: The True Story of Rosa Parks.* New York: Scholastic Inc., 2018.

Ruiz, Rachel. *When Rosa Parks Went Fishing.* North Mankato, MN: Picture Window Books, 2018.

Stoltman, Joan. *Rosa Parks.* New York: Gareth Stevens Publishing, 2018.

Internet Sites

Rosa Parks
www.womenshistory.org/education-resources/
biographies/rosa-parks

The Life of Rosa Parks
www.natgeokids.com/uk/discover/history/general-
history/rosa-parks/

Index